# Animal Headgear

Written by Brylee Gibson

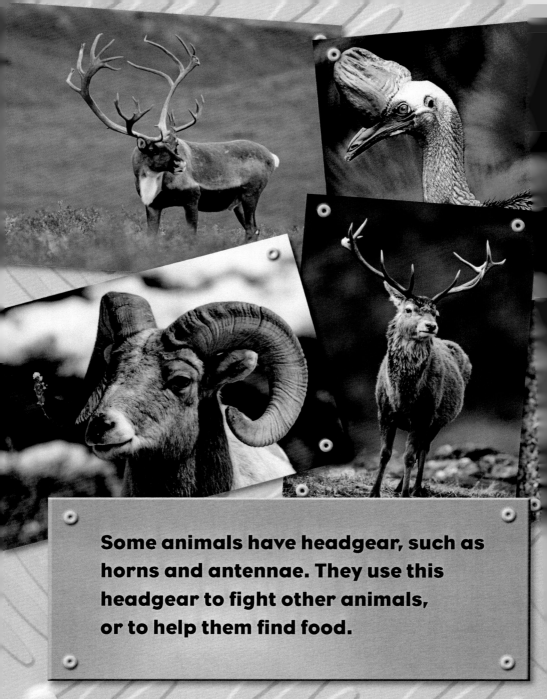

Some animals have headgear, such as horns and antennae. They use this headgear to fight other animals, or to help them find food.

Most animals keep the same headgear all their lives, but some can grow new headgear.

Some animals have horns on their heads that they use for fighting.

A bighorn sheep lives in the mountains. It has two big horns. It uses its horns to head-butt other sheep. It can head-butt all day.

A rhinoceros has one or two horns. The horns are very hard. The rhinoceros uses them to fight other rhinos.

**male caribou**

These animals have two long, curly horns. They will use their horns to fight each other and see who is the strongest. Because of their shape, the horns won't get stuck together when the animals fight.

Some animals have headgear
that they use for finding food.

This sea worm has a lot of antennae
on its head that are like a net.
They help the worm to catch food.

The worm can pull the antennae
inside its head and hide from danger.

antenna

A bison has two big horns.
It eats grass, but in winter the grass
can get covered up by snow.

The bison will use its horns like a shovel.
It will push the snow away
so that it can eat the grass.

This bird has a bony helmet
on top of its head. It can dig
a hole in the ground with the helmet
to find food.

This bird can't fly, so it uses the
helmet to push through trees, too.

**double-wattled cassowary**

Some animals have headgear that falls off.

A male deer is called a buck. Bucks have antlers for fighting. Every year the antlers fall off, but they will grow again and will be even bigger. They grow bigger and bigger every year.

Buck 1½ years old | Buck 2½ years old | Buck 3½ years old

This moose has antlers, too. Once a year it will fight other moose with its antlers. When the fighting is over, its antlers will fall off and it will grow some new ones. But the new antlers will be the same size.

# Headgear for fighting

# Headgear for finding food

## Index

# ▰▰▰ Guide Notes

---

**Title: Animal Headgear**
**Stage:** Launching Fluency – Orange

**Genre:** Non-fiction
**Approach:** Guided Reading
**Processes:** Thinking Critically, Exploring Language, Processing Information
**Written and Visual Focus:** Labels, Graph, Index, Fact Box
**Word Count:** 342

---

## THINKING CRITICALLY
(sample questions)
- Some animals have headgear such as horns and antennae on their heads. What do you know about animals' headgear?
- What might you expect to see in this book?
- Look at the index. Encourage the students to think about the information and make predictions about the text content.
- Look at pages 4 and 5. How do you think the rhinoceros might use its horns for fighting?
- Look at pages 10 and 11. What do you think could be some problems the bison might have when using its horns like a shovel?
- Look at pages 12 and 13. How do you know that this bird's helmet would have to be strong?
- Look at the graph on page 15. Why do you think the deers' antlers fall off and grow back again bigger?
- What in the book has helped you understand the information?
- What questions do you have after reading the text?

## EXPLORING LANGUAGE

### Terminology
Photograph credits, index

### Vocabulary
**Clarify:** antlers, horns, curly, antennae, shovel, helmet, bony
**Singular/Plural:** antenna/antennae, tree/trees, animal/animals, horn/horns
**Homonyms:** for/four, their/there, two/too/to

### Print Conventions
Apostrophes – contractions (won't, can't)